# Read and Play
# Noisy Machines

by Jim Pipe

Stargazer Books
Mankato, Minnesota

truck

A **truck** is noisy.
Rumble!

# motorcycle

A **motorcycle** is noisy. Vroom!

4

5

**drill**

A **drill** is noisy.

# lawnmower

A **lawnmower** is noisy.

7

**plane**

A jet **plane** is noisy. Roar!

digger

A **digger** is noisy.
Smash!

# fire engine

A **fire engine** is noisy.
Weeoh! Weeoh!

12

13

# steam train

A **steam train** is noisy. Chuff! Chuff!

15

**racing car**

16

A **racing car** is noisy. Brrm! Brrm!

# helicopter

A **helicopter** is noisy.
Chucka! Chucka!

18

19

# Who am I?

roar!

smash!

rumble!

vroom!

Match the sounds and pictures.

# How many?

Can you count the noisy machines?     21

# What noise?

**Ship**

**Ambulance**

**Rocket**

**Train**

Can you sound like these machines?

# Index

# For Parents and Teachers

## Questions you could ask:

*p. 2 What other noises might a truck make?* Think of a car, e.g. horn, brakes, starting up engine. Throughout the book, encourage the reader to make the noises of the different machines.

*p. 4 Can you see the engine?* Also point out the exhaust where noise comes out of the engine.

*p. 6 What noises do other tools make?* e.g. hammer, saw, electric drill, scraper.

*p. 8 Are machines noisier when they are close up?* Yes—compare the noise from a plane close up, e.g. at an airport, with the noise of a plane high in the sky.

*p. 10 What noises do things make when they break?* Ask the reader to think about the sounds made by different materials, e.g. wood splintering, glass cracking, plate smashing, clothes ripping.

*p. 12 Why does a fire engine have a noisy siren (and flashing lights)?* To tell other vehicles to let them through. Ask reader what other vehicles have a siren, e.g. ambulances, police cars/motorcycles.

*p. 17 What is that man doing?* Holding his hands over his ears to block out the loud sound. The other man is wearing earmuffs for the same reason.

*p. 18 What makes the sound on a helicopter?* The rotors make a whirring sound as they spin round and round. The rotors lift the helicopter into the air.

## Activities you could do:

• Get children to listen to sounds that machines make in classroom, e.g. whirring fan, sound of rolling wheels on hard surface, electric engine in household appliance.

• Role play: ask the reader to act out noises made by machine they are driving, e.g. getting in cab, starting engine, driving along, siren, brakes etc.

• Plan a day for children to bring in toy machines such as planes and diggers, and ask them to mimic the noises they make.

• Take children outside to listen for machine noises, e.g. traffic, lawnmower, or plane flying overhead.

© Aladdin Books Ltd 2009

**Designed and produced by**
Aladdin Books Ltd

**First published in 2009 in the United States by**
Stargazer Books,
distributed by
Black Rabbit Books
PO Box 3263
Mankato, MN 56002

Library of Congress Cataloging-in-Publication Data

Pipe, Jim, 1966-
  Noisy machines / Jim Pipe.
    p. cm. -- (Read and play)
  Includes bibliographical references and index.
  Summary: "In very simple language and photographs, describes loud machines such as motorcycles and construction drills. Includes quizzes and games"-- Provided by publisher.
  ISBN 978-1-59604-180-6
  1. Machinery--Noise--Juvenile literature. I. Title.
TJ179.P57 2009
428.1--dc22

2008015286

**Series consultant**
Zoe Stillwell is an experienced preschool teacher.

**Photocredits:**
l-left, r-right, b-bottom, t-top, c-center, m-middle
All photos from istockphoto.com except: 2-3, 20tl, 23br—Courtesy Mack Trucks, Inc. 22bl—Corbis.